the school of

HIS

PRESENCE

ERIC WILLIAM GILMOUR

SONSHIP

INTERNATIONAL

Copyright © 2017 by Eric William Gilmour

The School of His Presence
by Eric William Gilmour

Printed in the United States of America

All rights reserved. No part of this document may be reproduced or transmitted in any form, by any means (electronic,
photocopying, recording, or otherwise) without the written
permission of the author.

Unless otherwise indicated, Bible quotations are taken from
the New American Standard Bible (NASB). Copyright © 1960,
1962, 1963, 1968, 1971, 1972, 1973, 1975, 1977, 1995 by The
Lockman Foundation.

Scriptures marked (NKJV) are taken from the New King James
Version®. Copyright © 1982 by Thomas Nelson. Used by
permission. All rights reserved.

ISBN-13: 978-1724821881
ISBN-10: 1724821881

SONSHIP INTERNATIONAL
PO Box 196281
Winter Springs, FL 32707

"Bringing the Church into a deeper experience of God's presence in their daily lives."

Eric William Gilmour
Facebook/sonshipintl
Twitter@sonshipintl
Instagram@sonshipintl
YouTube/ewgilmour
sonship-international.org
eric@sonship-international.org

TABLE OF CONTENTS

THE SECRET OF HIS PRESENCE

In the secret of His presence,
how my soul delights to hide!
O, how precious are the lessons
which I learn at Jesus' side!
Earthly cares could never vex me,
neither trials lay me low;
For when Satan comes to tempt me,
to the "secret place" I go.
When my soul is faint and thirsty,
'neath the shadow of His wing
There is cool and pleasant shelter,
and a fresh and crystal spring;
And my Savior rests beside me
as we hold communion sweet;
If I tried, I could not utter
what He says when thus we meet.
Would you like to know the sweetness
of the secret of the Lord?
Go and hide beneath His shadow;
this shall then be your reward:
And whene'er you leave the silence
of that happy meeting place
You must mind and bear the image
of your Master in your face.

You will surely lose the blessing
and the fullness of your joy
If you let dark clouds distress you
and your inward peace destroy;
You may always be abiding,
if you will, at Jesus' side;
In the secret of His presence
you may every moment hide.

— Ellen L. Gorch[1]

---

[1] Ellen Lakshmi Gorch, "In the Secret of His Presence."

THE FELLOWSHIP
OF
HIS PRESENCE

"Rest. The only work you are
required to do now is to give your most
intense attention to His still, small voice within."
—Madame Guyon[2]

---

[2] Madame Jean Guyon, *A Short and Easy Method of Prayer; Praying the Heart of the Father* (Shippensburg, PA: Destiny Image Publishers, 2005).

"...the fellowship of the Spirit, be with you all."
— 2 Corinthians 13:14

Dear reader, if I were to ask you what God is after in your life, what would you say? Some would say obedience, faith, worship, love, or something along these lines. I believe all of these are right answers, but God has a more specific yearning in His heart. He has a burning desire to reproduce His Son through the dispensing of the Spirit of His Son into us.

God's joyful objective is to transform us into the image of His Son. And believe me, you want this too, for every aspect of your being was made to be mixed with God. Every problem in the human life can be traced back to one area or another that has not been mingled with God.

That is what the apostle Paul refers to when he writes, *"the image of His Son."* He uses such language only a few times in his writings. The first mention is in Romans 8:29: *"He predestined us to be conformed to the image of His Son...."* The heart of God's desire is clearly explained as transforming us into the *"image of the Son."* Jesus is to be *"the firstborn among many."* For in Hebrews

11

chapter 2 the writer states that God is *"bringing many sons to glory."*

What does *"the image of His Son"* mean? It means that Christ's very person is unobstructed while living through us. Another Scripture that uses such language tells us how this is going to happen. Second Corinthians 3:18 says, *"...beholding as in a mirror the glory of the Lord, [we] are being transformed into the same image from glory to glory, just as from the Lord, the Spirit."* It is plainly laid

"The image of His Son" means that Christ's very person is unobstructed while living through us.

out that the image of Jesus through our being, or the person of Christ united with our being, is the result of gazing upon the ever-increasing manifestation of God, who is the Lord Jesus Christ, experienced through the presence of the Holy Spirit. For sons are the perpetual recipients of God.

If, as Paul has plainly shown, beholding the glory is the only way to be transformed into the image of the Son, then not beholding His glory causes us to remain in our own image. This brings me to the reason why we emphasis the presence of God above everything else. The single most common question that I am asked, both in my travels and through social media, is, "How do I experience God?"

Many times I will give the inquirer a short answer like, "The experience of God is so rare because scattered minds are so common. You must get still." Or I'll respond with: "Just adore Him." The reason I can address the question with blanket statements like these is because our problem is a common one: We are a self-conscious people; everything in each of our individual little worlds revolves around us.

To give unto God all of our attention and affection will rip the soul away from the rule of self-consciousness and set it free to fly above the earth with God. Most people never soar in the heights because they are weighed down by the heaviness of self-rule. The soul's rebellion must be suffocated daily by wholehearted adoration through stillness. Oh mark these words in your soul; stillness is the antithesis of rebellion. Oh scattered soul, you have locked the gates into the glory of God.

So many of us go into prayer and never actually touch God because we did everything but adore Him. Many people's spiritual senses are numbed in the closet by all the pressure they put on themselves to be there and accomplish something. Our itch to accomplish something stems from our desire for something other than just Him.

Many have also asked, "How long should I pray?" Such a question is so difficult to answer because I know that man thinks clock while God thinks connection. We all have different lives and different schedules that God has entrusted to us in this life; some have more free time than others. Nevertheless, sitting with God is the most important thing in our lives.

A mother once wrote and rebuked me for encouraging people to spend large quantities of time with God. She felt condemned that she didn't have enough uninterrupted time to block out for just being with Him. Now, I don't mean to step on anyone's toes, but no matter how busy you are, you are never going to be as busy as Jesus was: the crowds came from all over to simply be where He was; the sick continuously pulled at Him; He was always with the twelve. Yet He still got up before the sun and went to a solitary place to be with God. Note these precious passages:

John 8:1 "Everyone went to his home but Jesus went to the Mount of Olives."

Luke 6:12 "It was at this time that He went off to the mountain to pray and He spent a whole night in prayer..."

Luke 4:42 "Jesus left and went to a secluded place."

Mark 1:35 "In the early morning, while it was still dark, Jesus got up, left the house and went away to a secluded place and was praying there."

Luke 22:39 "He proceeded to the Mount of Olives, as was His custom."

Luke 5:16 "Jesus often slipped away to the wilderness to pray."

Matthew 14:23 "He went up on a mountainside by Himself to pray..."

Luke 22:41 "He withdrew...and prayed."

Many people say that they have no time to sit in stillness and adoration before the Lord. But the funny thing is that they know a lot about "Dancing With The Stars," "Fantasy Football," "Home and Garden," or some other trending thing. The truth is that what we do with our time is an uncomfortable exposing of our true spiritual state.

One time a woman wrote a well thought out letter rebuking me for calling people to spend time alone simply worshipping God. She said that she didn't have an hour to herself. I thought to myself, with how long and well written this letter is, it must have taken her at least an hour to write. I guess that she had an hour to talk to me, but she hasn't an hour to talk with God?

We as humans will do almost anything to justify our staleness.

Backsliding is when your heart stops aching for His presence. Many of us are living in this state right now, so accustomed to our lukewarm hearts that any talk from a heart on fire with love is simply "impractical," "radical," or "wishful thinking." But dear friend, we must never cover the flame in our heart to comfort the ice in another's. We must call the church back to the Lover of her soul.

When I was in college at the Brownsville School of Ministry in Pensacola, Florida, it was easy to "live in the Glory." Not only did we live in the midst of an unparalleled sustained visitation of the Spirit, but we also had set aside our lives to just seek the Lord, learn the Scriptures, and preach the Gospel. We literally ate as little as we could and prayed as much as we could. Our bodies wasted away, our teeth broke, our skin was pale, our relationships dwindled, and we lost touch with modern society. It was like we had been frozen in time, as if we had created a bubble in which we set our faces to seek Him and nothing else. We were truly aliens in this world.

Of course this level of focused prayer and adoration was only for a season, and now everyone involved lives with pressing responsibilities, families, ministries, and relationships that we must steward. Even so, I remember working construction sometimes twelve hours a day in the Florida sun, coming home to a wife and daughter, and having little time to get alone with God. When I saw what my schedule was like, I had to make a decision to get up hours before the sun to sit with Him.

If I wasn't driving to the construction sites, I would sit in the back seat worshipping Jesus and meditating on the Scriptures. I would incorporate fasting into my life in ways that I could handle with my workload (i.e., every other day or three days a week to stay strong for manual labor). I would take some weekends and lock the door in my room to be alone from 4 a.m. to 4 p.m. so that I still had the late afternoon to help my wife and be with the kids.

Anytime my wife took the kids away to do something that I couldn't go to, I would literally stay in my closet every moment I was home, including all weekend. On top of these things, I would look at my schedule and find a three-day, seven-day, or sometimes ten-day window that I could block out, just to sit in my closet with a jug of water, to adore Him, to let Him lead me through the Scriptures.

The ecstasies and blissful life-changing encounters I had in those times are worth more to me than anything else in my life. During this time I would wake up early, spend time in adoration, and then come into the office earlier than anyone else to kneel down, at each person's chair, and pray for them. I would pray that they would fall in love with Jesus. No one knew, but it wasn't for them to know. I was burning with a desire to be faithful to the stewardship God had entrusted me with in that workplace, knowing that I have the power, privilege, and responsibility of God's ear.

In another season of life, I worked at Christ for all Nations; my days were long and I had a two-hour commute back and forth every day. It was my habit to skip lunch and lock myself in an empty office to simply adore Jesus. Sometimes, I stayed late or came in early, along with taking the commute time, to pray in the Spirit over some glorious worship music or feed my spirit man, listening to old messages from the voices of prophets.

Why am I telling you this? I only say these things to stir you to take your life of communion with God seriously and to make communion with God your life, and from that place to steward well whatever environment and relationships He has divinely situated for you at this present time of your life.

This is what matters. Not crowds and what most would call "results," but honest stewardship of what is divinely right before you.

I also want to encourage you that just because a daily experience of God has not been your life source up until now doesn't mean that it cannot be or that it is not supposed to be.

> **As you experience the sweetness of His presence more and more, it will swallow up your soul and all other interests will wither away.**

Concerning seeking the Lord, my dear friend Daniel Kolenda says, "Our seeking of the Lord is in exact proportion to our value of Him." He goes on to say that if you were offered $1 million to make a two-hour window every day to sit alone with God, you would find a way, simply because the value of that money is so great. If you value God Himself as the reward of seeking Him, you will cut out whatever you must in order to simply lay upon His chest and listen to His heart beat.

Remember that God is not responsible for an inconsistent experience of Him. Though discipline is the beginning, as you experience the sweetness of His presence more and more, it will swallow up your soul and all other interests will wither away. Delight will soon swallow discipline.

You never have to tell a couple that has fallen in love to make time to be with each other; it is all they think about. They simply live to be together, and to be apart from each other makes them feel as if they are each dying a slow, torturous death. If you have ever been in love, the real kind that robs you of any social existence, you know what I am taking about. In the same way, to be in love with Jesus means to love being with Him. Love causes delight to devour discipline.

COMING INTO HIS PRESENCE

PART 1

"Separation never comes from His side. He is always ready for communion with a prepared heart, and in this happy communion the bride becomes ever fairer, and more like her Lord. She is being progressively changed into His image, from one degree of glory to another, through the wondrous working of the Holy Spirit, until the Bridegroom can declare: Thou art all fair, My love; And there is no spot on thee. And now she is fit for service, and to it the Bridegroom woos her; she will not misrepresent Him…Union with Christ, and abiding in Christ, what do they not secure?
Peace, perfect peace; rest, constant rest; answers to all our prayers; victory over all our foes; pure, holy living; ever-increasing fruitfulness. All, all of these are the glad outcome of abiding in Christ."
—Hudson Taylor, *Union and Communion*[3]

---

[3] Hudson Taylor, *Union and Communion; The Marriage of Love Between Jesus and His Church* (Geanies House, Fearn, Great Britain: Christian Focus Publications, 1996).

*"... you were called into fellowship
with His Son."*
—1 Corinthians 1:9

Dear friends, everyone says, "God is all I want," but their lack of peace, joy, and contentment testifies against them. Everyone says, "I love Your presence." But you can tell how much someone really loves His presence by how uncomfortable they are when they are not aware of Him. Our schedule will testify more truly about what we love more than our mouths.

How do we spend our time? We can tell how much we love His presence by how dependent we are upon Him throughout our day. I want to write, step-by-step, how I experience the Lord every day. Though I know many of you reading this book already have deep relationships with God, I want to briefly walk through what I have found and believe to be the most important stages of prayer. Hopefully this will aid each of us in our daily experience of God.

The first stage in the soul that causes us to enter into an experience with God is *deprivation*. We must recognize our own personal depravity, meaning that we must recognize that it is impossible for us to make something happen when we are alone with Him. Our efforts are completely useless.

One of the ways we can recognize this poverty of spirit is relaxation. When we relax, our inward disposition testifies to God that we really are impotent in and of ourselves. To relax means that we recognize our personal bankruptcy and that all of our own efforts are worthless. So we give up or surrender. We must recognize our deep and utter helplessness and simply cast ourselves upon Him.

The second stage in the soul that causes us to experience God is what I would call *concentration*, which is another way of saying stillness. This is where we have, after recognizing our inability, collected ourselves and given ourselves completely to God. Stillness doesn't mean we cannot move. It means that the activity of the mind outside of fixation upon Him is stopped and the affections of the heart are centered on God Himself. It is removing all of our attention from lesser things and refusing to be interrupted by wayward thoughts.

Concentration, or stillness, is basically focusing all of one's attention upon God and away from other things. As we move into the next stage we will find that to be frozen in His sweetness is when the stillness we offer Him is swallowed by the stillness that comes from Him. God has this way about Him, as Psalm 65:7 describes: "...Who stills the roaring of the seas, the roaring of their waves and the tumult of the peoples."

Jesus, the exact representation of the Father, fulfilled this promise physically when the disciples were in turmoil on the sea. "He got up and rebuked the winds and the sea, and it became perfectly calm" (Matthew 8:26). So first we recognize our deprivation, and then, with humility, we can enter concentration, which prepares our hearts for the next stage.

The third stage we must enter into to experience God is *adoration*. This is the most important stage because the stages before lead up to it, and everything that comes after is a result of it. After the soul has recognized its poverty and focused itself in stillness, then and only then can it offer itself up as a complete offering to God. Adoration is incomplete until our souls are still.

Many of us have this problem: We are looking to the Lord while simultaneously worried about other things. We are split in two. There is no such thing as dualistic adoration. This is why men cannot touch Him, because Holy Spirit fire only falls on a whole sacrifice. Partial attentiveness will never receive the touch of God.

> **Adoration is not a state of mind; it is the preoccupation of the soul with the beauty of the Lord.**

The Scripture even states that, "You will seek Me and find Me when you search for Me with all your heart" (Jeremiah 29:13).

The first and greatest commandment given to us by Jesus and inscribed onto the heart of a man by the Spirit is, "Love the Lord your God with all your heart" (Matthew 22:37). Five hundred years before, David prayed that God would give him an undivided heart (Psalm 86:11). It is this wholehearted attentiveness that offers authentic adoration.

Adoration is not a state of mind; it is the preoccupation of the soul with the beauty of the Lord. It is the purest form of seeking God, opening the valve of our receptivity and enabling us to cling to God. Adoration is like air in the Kingdom of God.

This is the most indispensible element of the Christian life. It is both the enjoyment and the practice of our union with God, the exercise of our faith and the reception of His life, which empowers us to obey. Adoration is the beginning, sustaining, and end of all things in our union with God.

The fourth stage in the experience of God is *manifestation*. In adoration there will always be a manifestation of His presence. As we turn our attention to Him, it will take us like a river takes a yielded body. Oars are forbidden in the river of God (Isaiah 33:21).

When I first abandoned my life to the Lord in 1996, a man of God picked me up early in the morning for a road trip. As I sat there in the passenger seat, he turned to me and said, "Let's pray." I immediately started to rattle off in tongues, progressively getting louder with fervency and focus. Anyone looking at me would think I was in agony, rocking back and forth in constant motion.

This man of God waited patiently for me to finish machine-gunning God with tongues and desperate cries. When the smoke cleared from my war initiation with hell, the car became silent. Then with the steering wheel in one hand and his steaming coffee in the other, this man of God said softly, "Jesus, I worship You." He sat quietly and then said it again, "I worship You, precious Lamb of God." And in an instant, the whole car gradually filled with the undeniable presence of the Holy Spirit.

The tangible glory of heaven began to touch my soul. I was frustrated; I was infuriated; I was intrigued by how God's presence was invoked with so much ease. This man didn't raise his voice or even appeal to God to manifest Himself; he simply looked to Jesus in adoration. I learned an incredibly valuable lesson that day, namely, that adoration is the secret to experiencing the manifestation of His presence.

Oh dear reader, you must let this into your heart: a life of adoration is worth all the activity and power in the entire world. To gaze upon Him in sweet fixation and loving worship is more valuable to God than any spiritual gift or service. My favorite quote from A. W. Tozer would fit very well here, "When the eyes of the soul looking out meet the eyes of God looking in, heaven has begun upon the earth."[4]

This next stage is very important. Many people reach the stage of manifestation, but the fifth stage in experiencing God is what separates the men from the boys: it is the state of *resignation*, it is literally the fermentation of the sweetness of God's presence into wine. Fermentation takes time, a specific kind of time, time resigned to His presence.

As humans, we have a natural itch to move on, a desire for progress or momentum, but this robs so many people of the divine mixing of divinity with humanity. They are satisfied to touch and go. But resignation is lingering with Him, a simple acquiescence of oneself to the nothingness of God.

What do I mean by nothingness? This is when it seems that nothing is happening. The natural man is so fixed on activity that the nothingness of simple resignation to God's presence in still adoration is an irritation to him. We are addicted to activity and live by movement; therefore the still, sweet nothingness of God will always be nonsense to our natural human nature.

Too many of us wait for something to "happen" while we are in His presence without realizing that His

---

[4] A. W. Tozer, *The Pursuit of God* (Camp Hill, PA: Christian Publications, Inc., 1982).

presence is the happening. This stage of resigning to His presence will determine if you want anything other than just Him.

In a service at Brownsville Assembly of God in 1997, Lindell Cooley was leading worship. The service had broken into such a blissful, sweet, sustained time of corporate worship that he was moved to say a statement that has become a major part of my life and perfectly describes this stage of resigning to His presence. He said, "I don't want to offend God's Spirit by just rushing on."

> **To the degree that you only want Him, you will find such comfort and rest in the nothingness of simply looking at Him, just enjoying His nearness.**

To the degree that you only want Him, you will find such comfort and rest in the nothingness of simply looking at Him, just enjoying His nearness. Dr. Robert Gladstone once described this as "enjoying the covenant." Here is where many issues of the heart are settled.

To this day, I keep a notebook next to me when I sit with Him, to write down anything that He shows or speaks to me about Himself. In the beginning, I weighed the significance of my communion with Him by how full the paper was at the end of my time. I eventually recognized that this is not the case; everything God does is enduring but not always understandable. Or should I say, it is always indelible but not always intelligible.

Many times it could take weeks or even months to know what was actually happening to you as you stayed there in blissful adoration. We might leave without an intelligible speaking, but our hearts are soft and pliable from just enjoying contact with Him.

One time I was on a radio show that emphasizes signs and wonders. The host asked me about the most significant things that I had seen during extended times of seeking the Lord. I knew what kind of show it was and what they were actually pressing me to say, but my answer was essentially this: "I have seen incredible manifestations of all kinds, including visitations, visions, physical manifestations of gold dust, heavenly manna, oil, feathers, light flashes, sparks, and things such as supernatural deafness, being frozen in awe by the glory, tremors, shakings, surges of divine electric waves. But that thing which is most important to me is a lovesick, brokenhearted, pleasing pain in which my soul suffers out of satisfied longing for Him. This is where my heart becomes soft to obey the Lord. This is the most important thing to me, whatever way it comes about through His presence. This is all that matters — a heart that will obey God."

Once during my time with God, I was in this place of resignation, not looking to move on, but just feeling the bliss of His Person flow through my being. From this place of contentment, I entered into a vision: I was in a dark room and all I heard was a Voice say, "Do you want to know what is coming?" I knew, like all of God's questions, that the obvious answer is not normally the right one, so I thought about it. I finally answered, "No Lord. I just want You, because I know that if I have You, no matter what the future holds, I will be just fine."

This is what the resignation stage is all about — total contentment with God Himself. Above anything that He can do or will do — lead, instruct, and manifest — we want His presence. Borrowing language from David, the man after God's own heart, one thing I ask for; one thing I seek after: to live my life in the sweetness of His presence so that I may continually behold Him, inevitably resulting in me becoming like Him (Psalm 27:4, 8; 17:15).

Coming into His Presence

Part 2

"If Your presence does not go with us,
please do not lead us up from here."

"My presence will go with you and I will give you rest."

—Interaction between God and Moses,
Exodus 33:14-15

The sixth stage in the soul that experiences God's presence is what I call *inclination*. This is a spiritual urge in a particular direction. The leading of the Spirit that comes from a place of rest. Sometimes I call this the directive. These come in many ways, including visions, trances, instantaneous knowledge, overwhelming desires or leadings in the Scriptures, or themes in the Scriptures. However it comes, it issues from His sweet presence and person. Everything issues from His presence because this is the atmosphere of God's working. Even from the beginning of time, we see the presence of the Spirit hovering over the void before He spoke to restore it (Genesis 1:2).

The reason why it is so important to place resignation before inclination is because God only breathes into the soul that is detached from other motives and things. The resigned heart is the foundation upon which God will build. He may not lead in this way every time, but not to worry; we are only there for Him and His wishes anyway. When God called Moses to the top of the mountain, He simply called him to "be there." The apostles were called to first of all "be with Him."

Andrew Murray once wrote, "The presence of Christ was the training of the disciples."[5]

We must be jealous for His way, which means, His lead. If God doesn't do it, we must be content to live without it. As He leads, we follow. Communion with God is simply moving in concert with God, through God, into God, to live unto God.

Communion with God is simply moving in concert with God, through God, into God, to live unto God.

The seventh stage in the experience of God is *meditation*. As God grants to us His words, they must be unpacked, or as the psalmist wrote, "The unfolding of your words gives light" (Psalm 119:130). The definition of "fold" is concealing one part with another. That is exactly how God's voice is; one part conceals another. As we meditate upon God's directive, He will unfold and reveal it to us.

Meditation is holding His speaking in the light of His presence until it unfolds, revealing more light. Here is where God makes things intelligible, visible, communicable, and "prayable." For in His light we see light (Psalm 36). We must pray into the things God has shown us, especially the Scriptures He gives us. When we hold the Scriptures up to the light of God's presence in accordance with His directive, they suddenly come alive.

When His sweet presence has opened my eyes to see the wonderful things in His Word, I feel as if the pages themselves are breathing. I love to read the Scriptures in His presence because I am addicted to the electric thrill

---

[5] Andrew Murray, *The Secret of Spiritual Strength* (New Kensington, PA: Whitaker House, 1997).

of God's voice that comes through them. They are like the straw through which the honey of heaven flows. In this vein, I liken meditation to the suction by which we receive that honey.

Many times God gives men a reading pattern. What God has given me is a pattern to read one chapter from each of the Psalms, a proverb, a gospel, a prophet, a letter, and an Old Testament. I rarely ever get through the whole pattern, but I simply pick up where I left off. I am not in a rush because haste always muffles our ears. Everything is careful, deliberate, and important, so I take my time and read the Scriptures differently from any other reading that I do. I am much more interested in "hearing" than "learning."

It is important to note that being able to hear God through the Scriptures follows an already established overview of the whole redemptive plan as revealed in the entirety of the Scriptures. All of us must have these basic parameters. It doesn't take that long to establish them, but they are crucial to protecting us against deception.

The eighth stage for experiencing God is *intercession*. Intercession is standing before God on behalf of men. Whenever God shares His heart with us, it will produce in us inspired prayer. This is also directed by the Lord and wrapped in the sweetness of His manifested presence. He will share His sorrow with those who will come close enough to hear His heartbeat.

Leonard Ravenhill once said, "I would rather pray than be the greatest preacher in all the world."[6] Intercession is the surest sign of intimacy with God, for

---

[6] Leonard Ravenhill, "No Man Is Greater Than His Prayer Life," Audio Sermon, https://www.youtube.com/watch?v=M20aQ7ODuuw.

as a man draws near to God's heart, he will hear and feel what lies inside. Union with God is the merging of ecstasy and agony; the ecstasy of His presence and the agony of His heart. We pray out the things God has revealed in us.

Union with God is the merging of ecstasy and agony; the ecstasy of His presence and the agony of His heart.

The ninth stage is *revelation*. This is the unveiling of Jesus, who is so infinitely glorious that no part of His glory is ever repeated; He is like a constant waterfall of new life and new vision. Even what we think to be "old" is brand new in His presence because He makes all things new. In His presence, nothing can grow old or stale, dry or dead.

As He leads us into meditation, intercession, or a mix of both, we will find an unveiling of His person that is fresh and original. I have found while praying into the things God has specifically shown me that they expand far more than they did by meditation alone. I have also seen that as I intercede in concert with the Spirit, suddenly the inspiration in prayer unveils more of God's heart and intention.

Revelation is the means by which God transfers His substance into us. It is also the means by which we can transfer the glory we have seen to others. It is the means by which God will direct our praying in accordance with His divine plan. There is no substitute for the revelation of Jesus, for it shows us God's perfect Son and will in motion.

The tenth stage in the soul that experiences God is *impartation*. God literally dispenses Himself into us through revelation. This is so important: God makes us like His Son by revealing His Son, which imparts His

Son to us. The revelation of God is how we receive an impartation of God.

This impartation leads to the *transformation* of the inner man. Jesus Himself was transfigured through communion with God in God's presence, so our place of transformation will be no different. Such a transformation will cause an effortless *demonstration* of God's own life through our lives. A life that is animated by daily transformative experiences of God is a life being interwoven with His, that is to say, being renewed day by day, and being conformed into the image of God's dear Son.

There is no greater witness in this life than a God-filled man.

In conclusion, I submit to you that the means of such a demonstration is a divine transformation through an impartation that comes through a revelation of Jesus that will only come through the wonderful inclinations that happen in the resignation to His presence that we find in adoration, which is the beginning, the sustaining, and the end of our experiential union with God.

HIS PRESENCE
AND PERSON

*"It matters not how much we know of methods
or doctrines or power. What really matters is the
knowledge of the Son of God. Knowing God's Son
is the way, knowing God's Son is the truth,
and knowing God's Son is the life. Our power comes
from knowing His Son. All that God gives to us
is His Son, not a lot of things. Hence the whole
question lies in knowing God's Son."*
— Watchman Nee
Christ the Sum of all Spiritual Things[7]

---

[7] Watchman Nee, *Christ The Sum of All Spiritual Things* (New York: Christ Fellowship Publications, Inc., 1973).

"I am the way, the truth, and the Life..."
—John 14:6

If I said, "Jesus is our salvation," I don't know of any professing Christian that would offer a rebuttal. As a matter of fact, most would nod their heads in complete agreement without fully understanding what this statement actually means. Salvation is generally understood as being saved from sin and eternal damnation through accepting Jesus' sacrificial/substitutionary death on the cross. Such an understanding, though correct, still falls miserably short of what that salvation actually means.

"Jesus is our salvation" means that we have been saved from all the repercussions and the hell of a life without Jesus. Let me explain further. Jesus said, "I am the way," because He knew you and me. He knew that our propensity is to seek to find a way to serve Him and forget about Him. He knows that we as humans adopt religious devotion, morality, and good works as Christianity. He knows that we try to change our habits and live according to new, positive principles, claiming life through His saving power.

But Christianity is not a change of life but an *exchange* of life. Christianity is life for life. For the most part, most of us Christians have settled for a new belief system of morals connected with faith in God through Christ. We live in keeping with our new moral code and stamp Christ's name upon it, speaking our new religious language and steering clear of forbidden things, expecting the world to look at us and see Jesus. For too many of us, we make our own decisions and direct our own lives with our dos and don'ts, happy that we no longer live like the rest of the world who do not know or live by our newfound truths.

Have you ever considered that salvation means we have been saved from the worthless path that He never intended us to travel?

Dear reader, I fear that we have lost Jesus as the way where He literally directs us in His ways and leads us in His paths. "Jesus is the way" means that we have been saved from a life that is lived apart from the instruction of His presence and voice. Have you ever considered that salvation means we have been saved from the worthless path that He never intended us to travel?

Do you understand that our own way, living out of sync with God, is an evil thing (Isaiah 53:6)? It is very important to take this revelation to heart, because it is an evil thing to get out of step with God no matter how logical, productive, and wise our own way seems. There is a way that seems right to a man, but the end thereof is death (Proverbs 14:12).

Man's ways always lead to death, no matter how right they appear. Peter thought and spoke from a natural, human perspective and Jesus called him

Satan (Matthew 16:22-23). The mind of man is natural, earthly, and demonic (James 3:15). We need to regularly look to the Lord, humbly surrender our way, and trust Him to lead us as our literal Good Shepherd. Jesus must be our way.

Isn't it funny that Jesus saw Peter's plans as getting in front of Him (Matthew 16:23)? Jesus said, "I am the... truth," because He knows that men will cling to truths but forget Him who is the Truth. History shows us that the human way is to separate God from our practice unto Him.

We have a great blessing in the written Word, through which He has given us certain truths as guidelines for life in this world. But He never intended for us to learn them and practice them without His empowerment; He never intended for them to replace His presence. Rather, He wants to breathe and speak His very self into us through the things written.

I can't tell you how many times during street evangelism that I've come across that partier who knows more Scripture than I do or that homeless man who can quote the whole book of Galatians. These men only learned truths but they do not know Him who is the Truth. They only have a mental image of Christianity; they neither hear Christ nor see Him because there has been no life exchange.

Jesus said the same to the Pharisees who staunchly advocated the words of God with all their might and yet were unable to see the Word of God right in front of their faces. Jesus said to them, "You have neither heard His words nor seen His form" (John 5:37). Jesus teaches us through this that the spirit of religion is devotion to God without a living perception of Him.

Jesus was devoted to go through perceiving interaction with Him. Pilate asked Jesus the question, "What is truth?" (John 18:38). I believe Jesus was completely silent before him because if Pilate couldn't see the living Truth standing before him, no amount of lesser truths could help him. We have lost Jesus as the Truth and have replaced Him with truths. Because of this, men have judged their spirituality and nearness to God upon their knowledge of the Bible.

Dear friends, the Bible is only the means to bring us into a position of hearing His voice so that we may know Him. The words written must be written in us, and only His presence can perform such a wonder. It is true that God will not speak contrary to the Scriptures, but it is equally true that He speaks to us *through* the Scriptures in order for us to know Him who is the Truth.

Jesus said, "I am the...life," because He knows that everything, no matter how religious or spiritual, is absolutely lifeless without His presence. He knows that men seek to live their lives *for* Him without drawing life *from* Him.

I know that every single one of my failures was first the failure to let Christ be my life. This is the heart of the spirit of religion: "Give them everything but His presence." Why? Because only His presence gives life. This is why some hate religion and why others die under it; because it only gives a *picture* of Jesus but never introduces the *person* of Jesus. Without the presence of Him who is life there is only death.

Jesus laid down His life so that He might be our life. He gave His life to give life to those of us who give Him our lives, not just theologically, but in reality. Jesus is not just righteousness *for* us; He is righteousness *through* us. Many might deny this, but this is the way of the Spirit being animated by Christ Himself. He actually must be our quickening life, our state of being.

We have been saved from the life that we received from our natural fathers. After the fall, Adam reproduced after his own kind. Everyone lives from a defiled life source, defiled blood bent against God, towards self-preservation. Jesus came to rescue us from this selfish life by giving us His own life that is united with God's. As Leonard Ravenhill said, "Jesus didn't come to make bad men good, but to make dead men live."[8] Our doom is that without the life of Christ, we do not possess life in ourselves. "He who has the Son has life, and He who has not the Son has not life" (1 John 5:12).

Jesus is the Life, our divine animation, the righteous quick-ening of our being. So if you have been looking for the Way, look no further, for you can find it in Jesus, His presence and person. If you have been looking for the Truth, look no further, for it is Jesus, His presence and voice. If you are tired and worn out, lifeless and powerless, receive supernatural influence and strength from Jesus, for His presence and Word is the Life.

> **If you are tired and worn out, lifeless and powerless, receive supernatural influence and strength from Jesus, for His presence and Word is the Life.**

In conclusion, there are two questions in the eighth chapter of the book of John that the Pharisees ask Jesus that I believe expose the very heart of the spirit of religion. They asked Him, "Where is your Father?" and "Who are you?" Herein, I believe, lies the heart of the attack of the spirit of religion that is dominating people's lives, even in Christianity.

---

[8] Ravenhill, "No Man Is Greater Than His Prayer Life."

The question, "Where is your Father?" indicates a lack of awareness of God's presence, "Where...is...your Father?" The first issue with the religious is there is no perception of God's presence in their lives. The first attack of the spirit of religion on a believer is to cause them to have no real connection with God's presence. It is as if the enemy is saying, "Keep everything going, practices, language, songs, schedule, devotions, just don't let them experience God's presence."

The second question, "Who are you?" follows a lack of God's presence simply because it is the means by which Jesus is revealed. The religious person has no real revelation of the person of Jesus. The heart of the attacks on the Christian life is a revelation of Jesus.

The unveiling of the Son is everything. True Christianity is a revelation of Jesus. If the enemy can block your vision of Jesus, you will remain blind and unable to walk with God. For any true walk with God is an endless vision of Jesus. In conclusion, it is important to note that the spirit of religion has these main areas of attack, "Where is your Father?" and "Who are you?"

SEVEN-DAY DEVOTIONAL

DAY ONE

I once met with a good friend for lunch. We had an interesting conversation. He stated that many find God in different ways. That for some people they do not need silence to hear His voice, or they must use other means by which to experience God, such as fishing, running, or other things. He stated that not everybody needs to get alone to experience God. But I suggest to you that, even if this is true, these people can only go so deep. And though it is all fine and well that they find God this way, the truth of the matter is that man can possess as much of God as He wants.

Individuals like this seem to have a plethora of other interests. And most of the time they do not know what God is saying. Nor are they familiar with the sweetness of His voice and presence, or the step-by-step precepts and directions/instructions of God are little known to them. You will find it to be this way in every case. For man must enter his closet, shut the door, and pray to the Father who sees him in secret.

Jesus as the pattern Son woke up before the dawn and found a solitary place. He, when everyone else went to their homes, met with God on the mountain. Sons live by receiving God's life in private. Their public life is rooted in their private experience. The truth is, dear, scattered, noisy brother, you can live the way that you are living, but you will remain where you are. You will not behold, in depth, the glory of the Lord that transforms you from glory to glory.

When God became a man and His disciples longed to experience God the way that He did, He specifically taught them how, "Go into your closet and shut the door...." Silence and solitude are God's idea, not man's idea. As Thomas Dubay once stated, "It is the overstimulation that kills the receptivity of our souls."[9] A wise man once stated, "Perhaps the reason why we so often cannot abide in silence is that we fear that it should make more apparent the absence rather than the presence of truth in ourselves."

I once heard a man tortured for Christ say, "The prerequisite for apprehending God is silence. The radio and TV have to be switched off...many souls never find the silent God because of much noise in their homes...I have traveled around the world, but the most interesting journeys have been those I made in silence in the depths of my own heart, the only place God wishes to meet me." As Madame Guyon wrote, "God dwells in infinite stillness...."[10] Let us join Him there.

---

[9] Thomas Dubay, "Contemplation," Audio Sermon, https://www.youtube.com/watch?v=KsZ9TpZ16n4.
[10] Guyon, *A Short and Easy Method of Prayer; Praying the Heart of the Father.*

DAY TWO

"As soon as you come into the presence of God...remain there in His divine presence without being troubled about a subject for prayer. Simply enjoy God. Cease all activity, lest God's presence is diminished by your activity. Seek nothing from God during this quiet moment except to love Him..."
—Madame Guyon[11]

This is a golden key to the experience of God. David shares the same secret in Psalm 62:1, "My soul waits in silence for God alone." He is not waiting for something from God. He is looking to God Himself; the very person of God, which is to say His very presence and His very voice. His concern isn't the outward decibels as much as the inward decibels of the soul. His mind and will and emotions are quieted and still, waiting for God. We must understand the value of what he is saying.

To the degree your eyes are waiting for something other than God, you will miss Him. If your mind is scattered and spread thin on so many things, you will

---

[11] Madame Jean Guyon, *Experiencing God Through Prayer* (New Kensington, PA: Whitaker House, 1984).

miss Him. If your will is bent against God and wanting other things, then you will miss Him. If your affections are clouded by looking for other things to satisfy and desire, you will miss Him. David gives us the key to receiving God; it is waiting upon the Lord with a still, quieted soul that looks for God alone.

Madame Guyon expounds on this very thought with perfection, saying, "Simply enjoy God. Cease all activity.... Seek nothing from God during this quiet moment except to love Him."[12] One of my favorite quotes from Witness Lee is, "The more we enjoy God the more we know Him."[13] Rest and enjoy Him, for in the reception of this honey, all the nutrients needed to obey God are received.

---

[12] Guyon, *Experiencing God Through Prayer*.

[13] Witness Lee, *How to Enjoy God and How to Practice the Enjoyment of God* (Anaheim, CA: Living Stream Ministries, 2006).

DAY THREE

"If ever the passions of the soul become turbulent,
a gentle retreat inwards to a present God easily
deadens and pacifies them."
—Madame Guyon[14]

This is one of my favorite quotes of all time. It has probably helped me more than any other quote I have ever read in my life. Simply because the passions of the soul have this way about them—they are turbulent. They are wild and scattered.

As C. S. Lewis said, "The soul will fight tooth and nail to say alive."[15] Madame Guyon shows us the secret to a life that is "not by might nor by power but by the Spirit." It is the Romans 8:11 (put to death the deeds of the body by the Spirit) truth practically unveiled for us. "A gentle retreat inwards...." This speaks of not trying to directly address or fight against the passion or turbulence, but rather an encouragement to retract from them that we may extract from Him.

---

[14] Guyon, *A Short and Easy Method of Prayer; Praying the Heart of the Father.*
[15] C. S. Lewis, *Mere Christianity* (New York: Touchstone, 1943).

We are to pull back away, retreat from the issue to "a present God" that is the reality of the presence of God in your heart. Literally to stop and give all of your adoration and attention to Him, which will always awaken your consciousness of Him. The sweet empowering presence of God will, with great ease, exercise His superior power and deaden and pacify these cravings and passions for sin and self-centeredness.

This is how we put to death the deeds of the flesh by the Spirit. Not with our own power, but with the power of God's Spirit, who is the presence of God in the world today. A gentle retreat inwards to a present God will easily deaden and pacify our passions and make Spirit-wrought holiness the fruit of our lives. Holiness is the fruit of being addicted to the maximum pleasure of life, which is God Himself.

DAY FOUR

*"God cannot give us peace and happiness apart from
Himself because there is no such thing."*
—C. S. Lewis[16]

In Psalm 119 David writes, "The Lord is my portion."
How many times have we all heard this statement?
Though it can easily lose its meaning through overuse
and light-hearted clichés, it is an incredibly powerful
statement. It is my opinion that this is the heart of the
issues in the church. Let me explain by unpacking this
phrase for us.

What does "my portion" mean? It means that which
is personally given to me. That which is mine. It is
freely, rightfully mine by gift. What is freely, rightfully,
personally ours by gift? The Lord Himself. Not just an
attribute of His, not just a power of His, not just a thing
that He may have, but He Himself. The Lord Himself is
your portion. He gives Himself to us freely; not just His
things, but very self.

---

[16] C. S. Lewis, "Good Reads," https://www.goodreads.com/
quotes/863496-god-cannot-give-us-a-happiness-and-peace-
apart-from.

As He gives Himself to us we receive all that He is. Notice also that it does not say, "the Savior is my portion," or "the Healer is my portion," but "the Lord is my portion." This is important because in the Lordship of Christ is the only passage into the receiving the free gift of Him. If we will not have Him as the reigning King in our lives, then we will not be able receive Him as our portion.

The last point is this little word *is*. This means that He was not just our portion in the past nor in the future, but rather in the present moment that we are in the Lord is our portion. He, in this very moment that you are in, is eagerly desiring to give Himself to you. As we remain under His Lordship as King and continuously receive God as the all-inclusive life supply, we find indescribable love, joy, peace, and the ability/desire to obey Him and be like Him in this life.

Day Five

*"I am the Light of the world; he who follows Me will
not walk in darkness, but will have the Light of life."*
—Jesus Christ, John 8:2

I once asked my daughter, who was eight years old at
the time, what does it really mean to follow Jesus? I
wanted her childlike, simplistic perspective. She said to
me three simple things that I believe were inspired by
the Spirit of God. The first thing that she said is that in
order to follow Jesus I must look at Him. This may seem
very elementary, but what it implies is relevant to more
than a few.

First, I can't look at other people, circumstances,
situations, victories, my track record, or any other thing.
If I am to ever follow Him, I must keep my attention
upon Him. If ever these things take our eyes off of Him,
it becomes incredibly difficult to follow Him. I would
venture to say, it is impossible to follow Him if we are
not looking unto Him. As a matter of fact, the Scripture
states, "looking unto Jesus, the author and finisher of
our faith" (Hebrews 12:2, NKJV). The Lord authors and
brings our faith to completion by this means, looking
unto Him.

My dear friend Michael Koulianos always says, "In order to love Him constantly, my heart must see Him constantly." So if your heart is holding on to offenses, judgments, or competition and comparison, your eyes have left Him. In order to look upon another, I must remove my gaze from upon Him.

Let me encourage you with this; give all of your attention to Jesus and only Jesus. Let His voice mean everything to you. Be moved by, inspired by, directed by, and empowered by His voice and His opinion alone. Remember when Jesus told Peter what was going to happen to him in the future? Peter responded to the Lord by asking about John. Jesus' answer to him is completely fitting in this first point in following Him. He said, "Don't worry about John; you follow Me."

Jesus shows us here that it is impossible to follow Him if we are concerned, competing, comparing, and preoccupied with someone else or something else. A. W. Tozer, in one of his classic lines, said that our lives should be an endless preoccupation with God Himself. So let us follow Jesus by fixing our eyes on Him alone.

Day Six

Yesterday we looked at the fact that in order to look at something else, we must first take eyes off Jesus. In order to follow Jesus, we must first look to Him. The next point, childlike as it is, is very important and follows keeping our eyes upon Jesus. It is simple; we must get behind Him. You cannot follow someone standing in front of them. You cannot follow someone standing beside them. In order to follow someone, you must be behind them.

The very phrase, "Follow Me" implies getting behind. Many of us want to head in front of Him and have Him follow us, but I remember hearing a preacher say, "Jesus did not die so that He may follow you." The Holy Spirit is not like Casper the Friendly Ghost who goes with you everywhere you go. The Lord is with you everywhere He goes.

It is imperative that we remain behind Him, following each step. Remaining in rhythm. Synchronized with His movements. This is the experiential fellowship and experiential union overflowing into everyday life. There are many people who believe that following Jesus means walking beside Him and reasoning with Him along the way. Our input is no good. Our intellect is too low to align with the higher divine way of God.

John Ruusbroec once wrote, "Reason is site by a created light, while revelation is cited by the uncreated light."[17] We must have His divine supernatural Spirit-inspired/empowered directive. We cannot live stooping so low as to trust in our own intellect and brilliance. For His ways are higher than our ways and His thoughts are not our thoughts.

Remember in the Scriptures when Peter had in mind the plans of men and not the plans of God, though they seemed to be in the interest of the Lord? Jesus rebuked him and said, "Get behind Me" (Matthew 16:23, Mark 8:33). Jesus forever settled the fact that the way of man is in line with Satan, who seeks to step in front of the Lord.

The way of man, human ingenuity, is stepping in front of the Lord. We must recognize that if we trust in our own way and are not subject to living our lives behind Him, He has only one thing to say to us, "Get behind Me." It is satanic to get out from behind Him. We must live every day of our lives subjected to His divine rule.

---

[17] John Ruusbroec, *The Spiritual Espousals* (Mahwah, NJ: Paulist Press, 1985).

DAY SEVEN

The third and final point of this childlike perspective of what it is to follow Jesus is remaining in a place of looking unto Jesus and being subjected to Him. Jesus says, "I am *the true vine*" (John 15:1, emphasis added). He says, "true vine" because there are many other kinds of vines out there that a man can choose to seek to draw his life from. But the only one that is true, or shall I say, real or alive, is the person of God in Jesus Christ through the presence of the Spirit.

Jesus goes on to say, "*abide* in Me..." (John 15:4, emphasis added). The word "abide" has to do with remaining. Just because we have looked to Him in the past and just because we have been subjected to Him in the past doesn't automatically mean that we are looking unto Him or subject to Him at this current time. But to abide in Him is to refuse to depart from Him. To abide in Him is to cling to Him.

We abide by clinging and we cling to abide. There isn't a more clear call to remain in His presence like the command to follow Him. When Jesus says, "Follow Me," He is saying, in a sense, "Do whatever you must to remain in My presence." It means abide, stay near Me, looking at Me, behind Me, stay here in stride with Me, synchronized with Me step-by-step.

If we go ahead, we are not led. But the sons of God are led by the Spirit; they do not go ahead of the Spirit. They are subjected to the Spirit of Jesus Christ. So let us follow Jesus, by a life that chooses to remain in His presence continually, because He is our life supply. Many of the old-time writers used to say a phrase that I love so much that encapsulates this whole cry of dependency, "Oh, Life of my life."

Speak, Lord, in the Stillness

Speak, Lord, in the stillness,
While I wait on Thee;
Hushed my heart to listen,
In expectancy.
Speak, O blessed Master,
In this quiet hour;
Let me see Thy face, Lord,
Feel Thy touch of power.
For the words Thou speakest,
They are life indeed;
Living bread from heaven,
Now my spirit feed!
All to Thee is yielded,
I am not my own;
Blissful, glad surrender,
I am Thine alone.
Speak, Thy servant heareth,
Be not silent, Lord;
Waits my soul upon Thee
For the quickening word.
Fill me with the knowledge
Of Thy glorious will;
All Thine own good pleasure
In Thy child fulfill.

Like a watered garden,
Full of fragrance rare,
Lingering in Thy presence,
Let my life appear.

—Emily May Grimes (1868-1927)[18]

---

[18] Emily Grimes, "Lord, Speak in the Stillness," Hymnary. org., https://hymnary.org/text/speak_lord_in_the_stillness.

ABOUT THE AUTHOR

Eric and Brooke Gilmour

Sonship International is a ministry started by Eric and Brooke Gilmour, seeking to bring the church into a deeper experience of God in their daily lives while preaching the Gospel throughout the world. Graduate of the Brownsville Revival School of Ministry, Eric conducts The School of His Presence in the United States and abroad. Eric is a conference speaker and author of the books *Burn, Union, Into the Cloud, Divine Life, Enjoying the Gospel,* and *The School of His Presence,* and *Nostalgia.*

NOTES

_____
_____
_____
_____
_____
_____
_____
_____
_____
_____
_____
_____
_____
_____
_____
_____
_____
_____
_____
_____
_____
_____
_____
_____
_____
_____
_____

BIBLIOGRAPHY

Dubay, Thomas. "Contemplation." Audio Sermon. https://www.youtube.com/watch?v= KsZ9TpZ16n4.

Gorch, Ellen Lakshmi. "In the Secret of His Presence."

Grimes, Emily. "Lord, Speak in the Stillness." Hymnary. org. https://hymnary.org/text/speak_lord_in_ the_stillness.

Guyon, Madame Jean. *A Short and Easy Method of Prayer; Praying the Heart of the Father.* Shippensburg, PA: Destiny Image Publishers, 2005.

Guyon, Madame Jean. *Experiencing God Through Prayer.* New Kensington, PA: Whitaker House, 1984.

Lee, Witness. *How to Enjoy God and How to Practice the Enjoyment of God.* Anaheim, CA: Living Stream Ministries, 2006.

Lewis, C. S. "Good Reads." https://www.goodreads. com/quotes/863496-god-cannot-give-us-a-happiness-and-peace-apart-from.

Lewis, C. S. *Mere Christianity.* New York: Touchstone, 1943.

Murray, Andrew. *The Secret of Spiritual Strength.* New Kensington, PA: Whitaker House, 1997.

Nee, Watchman. *Christ The Sum of All Spiritual Things.* New York: Christ Fellowship Publications, Inc., 1973.

Ravenhill, Leonard. "No Man Is Greater Than His Prayer Life." Audio Sermon. https://www.youtube. com/watch?v=M20aQ7ODuuw.

Ruusbroec, John. *The Spiritual Espousals.* Mahwah, NJ: Paulist Press, 1985.

Taylor, Hudson. *Union and Communion; The Marriage of Love Between Jesus and His Church.* Geanies House, Fearn, Great Britain: Christian Focus Publications, 1996.

Tozer, A. W. *The Pursuit of God.* Camp Hill, PA: Christian Publications, Inc., 1982.

Additional Books by Eric Gilmour

In the School of His Presence

Burn: Melting into the Image of Jesus

Union: The Thirsting Soul Satisfied in God

Into the Cloud: Becoming God's Spokesman

Enjoying the Gospel

Divine Life: Conversations on the Spiritual Life

Nostalgia

Available on:
Amazon, Nook, Kindle, Kobo, iBooks

BURN

God is raising up mystical wonder workers who seek oneness with God through surrender and bleed deliverance to this sin sick world. In this book lies the pillars to becoming the Jesus people in the earth today — hose who manifest the Person of Christ through character, power and wisdom.

Available on:

Amazon, Nook, Kindle, Kobo, iBooks

UNION

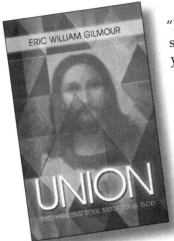

"If you come to Him for something other than Him, you will miss Him."

"Men are bent against pleasure in the Spirit to the degree that they don't experience it."

The Christian life that isn't satisfied with God alone, testifies to the world that God isn't enough."

"Part of the reason most Christians are not eager to give people what they have, is because what they have doesn't satisfy them."

In *Union*, Eric W. Gilmour explains the relationship God desires to have with every believer. It is up to you to initiate your part in His planned "Union" with Him.

Available on:

Amazon, Nook, Kindle, Kobo, iBooks

INTO THE CLOUD

"The prophet has become his message. He does not prepare messages, he speaks what has been spoken into him; he speaks what has been spoken into him; he speaks what he himself has become." "Obedience is when a man's life is yielded to the extent that God can perform through that man the things He has spoken to him." "We must seek to find Christ present in the depths of the scriptures, not merely as type and shadow, but as the living word, the present speaking of God."

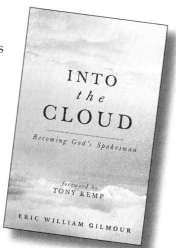

Available on:

Amazon, Nook, Kindle, Kobo, iBooks

ENJOYING THE GOSPEL

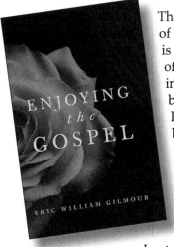

The Gospel is the offering of God's presence to men. It is the invitation into a life of experiencing Him. The inspiration of our lives must be our past experiences of Him; our satisfaction must be our present experience of Him; our hunger is for our future experiences of Him. I would much rather touch Him than attempt to define Him. I would rather move Him than seek to simply understand Him. I would rather know Him than merely perform His works.

Are you with me?

Let us live our lives enjoying this glorious Gospel!

Available on:

Amazon, Nook, Kindle, Kobo, iBooks

DIVINE LIFE

This book has been compiled from conversations on the Spiritual Life between Eric Gilmour, Michael Dow and David Popovici.

Available on:

Amazon, Nook, Kindle, Kobo, iBooks

NOSTALGIA: GOD'S BROKEN HEART

God's heart is broken as His people look to other things for satisfaction, joy and peace. He is not willing to let them go. He relays His anguish through Hosea, the brokenhearted prophet. In this prophetic book lies the core speaking of God to the Western world. Wrought with divine nostalgia, God calls His people to solitude with Him that He may whisper into their ears and be their deliverance and all satisfying lover. Though others cried, "injustice" Hosea cries, "You don't love me anymore."

Available on:

Amazon, Nook, Kindle, Kobo, iBooks

34667087R10049

Made in the USA
Middletown, DE
02 February 2019